Allon

Books 1-9
STUDY GUIDE

Shawn Lamb

Allon Books

PARENT STUDY GUIDE FOR ALLON – BOOK 1-9 by Shawn Lamb
Published by Allon Books
209 Hickory Way Court
Antioch, Tennessee 37013
www.allonbooks.com

Cover design by Robert Lamb

International Standard Book Number: 978-0-9891029-6-4

Preface

I'm humbled that God has led you to include these books in your teaching. The Great Teacher, Our Lord Jesus, used parables (allegory) to instruct His audience. My simple stories do not and cannot rise to His level of richness; only to allow Him to use my finite imagination in a fun way to convey spiritual principles.

There are numerous ways human allegory can be interpreted. The purpose of this booklet is to explain my thoughts and intentions with the stories; how I use characters, mortals and immortals, to illustrate the theme(s) of the individual books; and give suggested questions. Still, each parent should use this guide as best suits their child/children to develop understanding of Biblical Truths. Perhaps a good way to start is by explaining what allegory is, thus laying the foundation for instruction.

Blessings and Enjoy!

Shawn Lamb

Table of Contents

Allon

Book 1

CRUITHEAR   DIONADAIR

RIGA

Shawn Lamb

Book 1 - Overview

THE OVERARCHING SPIRITUAL THEME is about relationships. In the story, I strive to make comparisons and contrasts of relationships based upon Scripture. Some characters may represent archetypes; others show correlations of the theme by their actions and reactions.

Naturally, the first and foremost relationship is to Jor'el (God). How the characters interact with the Almighty is critical to their behavior and dealings with each other. Whenever Jor'el is present it is in a cloud-masked haze. Although Jesus came to earth in the flesh, God abhors graven images, so Jor'el is never clearly seen yet his presence is everywhere.

The second key relationship is between Ellis and Shannan. Too many YA fiction books are about dysfunctional relationships and portraying young men and women engaged in improper partnerships. I chose to be different, and based Ellis and Shannan on Biblical principles outlined in Ephesians and Proverbs. Situations will never cross the line in any of my books whether YA fantasy or adult historical. Still, I tackle hard issues and the serious consequences resulting from wrong moral choices.

Never do the protagonists use magic or possess magical weapons. This is a choice I made to show that it is through incidents requiring faith, skill, intellect and courage, the characters grow, mature, learn their strengths and weaknesses and either succeed or fail. The supernatural is relegated to where it belongs, with the immortal beings. This leads to another relationship I explore, Guardians and Shadow Warriors.

6

Guardians and Shadow Warriors represent holy angels and fallen angels. I chose to use the term *fallen angels* rather than demons, since I keep the Shadow Warriors pretty much in their original state—physical perfection, though their spirits altered by darkness—and not some grotesque creatures lurking about.

Ephesians 6:12
For we wrestle not against flesh and blood, but against principalities, against powers, against the rulers of the darkness of this word, against spiritual wickedness in heavenly places.

Shadow Warriors and Guardians bring the spiritual battle into the physical realm. Various Scripture references tell of angels having feelings, being intelligent, wise, curious and powerful along with a hierarchy to their ranks. I incorporate all these facets into Shadow Warriors and Guardians, but they are not angels in totality. They have distinct personalities and character traits that sometimes show fallibility. I also limit their power in physical form, so it is not their supernatural abilities that constantly rescue or vex mortals. Through their eyes I explore the frailties and machinations of mankind. For the Guardians, mortals can be a source of amazement and disappointment. For Shadow Warriors, mortals are weaklings to be dominated.

The Characters in Book 1
Central to the Theme

ELLIS typifies the Promised Prince, and in many ways exhibits Christ-like symbolism. He is born to be king, struggles against temptations, encounters danger, proves his identity, gains his armor for the battle to come, is *presumed* dead and returns to save his bride and kingdom. His reliance on Jor'el (God) is paramount to his success or failure. Such is the case with all of us as Believers.

I use Ellis' journey to highlight Christian virtues and worldly temptations by his interactions with various people he meets along the way. The armor serves as it does in Scripture (Eph. 6:13-18), as a figure for how we are to stay equipped and protected for our task.

With Ellis' relationship to Shannan, I show him learning and growing as outlined in Ephesians 5:25-33, where husbands are instructed on how to treat their wives. Even though not married, he and Shannan are destined to be together. The principles in Ephesians can be used as a general rule for instructing young men on how they should treat young women, as a precious gift from God—a sister in Christ to be respected, her reputation protected and her spiritual life encouraged.

SHANNAN is a representation of the bride of Christ in the pure sense. She is strong, and physically and spiritually well armed for her mission. She can act independently of Ellis, assume leadership when needed and face down a Guardian or Shadow Warrior. However, she doesn't need to prove anything. Rather she is self-confident in her role appointed by Jor'el, which allows her to support Ellis without anger, question or resentment of his role. I use her to show young women that there is beauty in a submissive spirit, not weakness. Proverbs 31 says the value of a virtuous woman is above the price of rubies, and as such, her husband—or this case Ellis—can safely trust her. I use the relationship to show a proper balance of mutual dependency based upon love (*agape*) that seeks the spiritual and physical betterment of the other, not to dominate or intimidate.

SIR NILES, Shannan's grandfather, is a father figure in the faith. He equipped Shannan for her role and aided Ellis in the last part of his preparation and during his journey. He is simply the elder teaching the younger.

MARCELLUS typifies man's driving ambition to rule. He neither fears Jor'el nor the Dark Way. He is totally controlled by his lust for power. Like all men of such an ilk, it is too late when he realizes the truth. He was never blind to reality, rather chose to ignore it (Proverbs 12:15a & Proverbs 16:18). However, his actions have horrible repercussions upon his brother Hugh and his family.

DARIUS models the friend who sticks closer than a brother (Proverbs 18:24b). Although raised to believe he and Ellis were related, Darius' tenacious spirit and love for Ellis carries him through the story. Along the way, situations test his endurance and personal faith.

ERIN serves as a counter to Shannan by her impulsive actions. Despite the hardship and tragedy her family suffers, she is a woman of passion, not faith. This leads her to tempt Ellis. His refusal makes her recoil and grow bitter. A series of events challenges her faith and perspective, until again, her impulsiveness makes a desperate choice. Unlike the thoughtlessness of earlier, this time it is self-sacrificing, showing the growth and change of a person for the better (Philippians 2:3-4).

KEMP is the skeptic, the scoffer, the unbeliever; who even when he sees the truth in front of him, refuses to acknowledge it. No, he is not Judas, though some may argue similarities. Judas played the role of a believer in Jesus. Kemp never fully embraced Ellis' birthright and met everything with contention. He went along for self-preservation. His weaknesses allow him to be manipulated, but, ultimately, he makes his own choice. (1 John 2:19)

LATHAM is the man who allies himself with evil. In fact, being Dagar's son illustrates Jesus' scolding of the Pharisees.

John 8:44

"You are of your father the devil and the lust of your father you will do."

Still, Latham does not possess or have natural magical power. The talisman serves as the conduit for Dagar to unleash *his* supernatural powers. In this, Latham is merely the physical stand-in for Dagar. His whole purpose is to see his father released and bring Allon into total darkness.

DAGAR is Lucifer in his perfect beauty and powerful form (Ezekiel 28:12-19 & Isaiah 14:12-17). I made a conscious choice not to make Dagar dark and satanic in appearance like most supernatural beings in fantasy. Like Lucifer, Dagar was in an exalted position before pride consumed him and he fell. Shadow Warriors are those Guardians who followed him, or he coerced.

KELL is a depiction of Michael, the top archangel. He is the most powerful Guardian, wise and dedicated to his duty to Jor'el and the mortals of Allon. Each Guardian has a certain responsibility, thus a power(s) to match. (*These powers will be explored in other books.*) The fallibility of the Guardians is what makes them likeable and not stiff in their interaction with mortals as seen in other fantasies. Often I use Guardians to verbalize spiritual truth.

10

Even in the secondary characters, I show various Biblical and spiritual truths in the decisions they make.

For example: **ALLARD, LORD OF THE MEADOWLANDS** and Member of the Council of Twelve. He is a shrewd and practical man, who by helping Ellis in a show of worldly fealty comes face-to-face with a spiritual choice. Ellis' answer to Allard's question of "What do you want?" is key to all people of all times:

"I'm Jor'el's chosen. Latham is of the Dark Way. It is between those two you must choose. Anything less than a clear choice is as difficult as maintaining your balance on a fence. You may survive for a while, but at some point you will fall to one side or the other. It would be best by choice and not by accident."

When faced with the truth of Jesus Christ, a choice must be made, there is no gray area, and there is no fence. People delude themselves into believing there is a middle ground where Scripture is exclusive.

John 14:6
I am the Way, the Truth and the Life; no man comes unto the Father but by Me.

Thus all my characters—main and secondary—must make a choice.

Suggested Questions
Allon - Book 1

(Feel free to make your own questions.)

1. Who is Jor'el?
2. Describe Ellis' character. Who in Scripture does he remind you of and why?
3. In what ways was he tested? Why? And who administered the tests?
4. Do you understand about spiritual armor?
5. Describe Shannan's character. How does she relate to Ellis?
6. What can you learn from their relationship?
7. What action did Erin take to confuse Ellis? What made her change?
8. What made Kemp change his mind about Ellis? How did this affect his later choice to aid Latham?
9. Give a reason(s) why Marcellus agreed to Latham's plan against Ellis?
10. How did Marcellus' actions impact his brother Hugh? Can your personal sin affect others?
11. What Biblical being does Dagar remind you of?
12. What is Latham's relation to Dagar?
13. What are Guardians and Shadow Warriors?
14. To whom does Ellis show mercy at the end?

Allon

Book 2

Insurrection

Shawn Lamb

Allon Books

Book 2 - Overview

T HIS BOOK PARES DOWN FROM THE EPIC SCOPE of Book 1 to a more personal story. Ellis faces his first challenge as king: an insurrection stirred in an act of revenge by Musetta. She was a minor character in Book 1, but now takes on the major villain's role. It is rare to have a female villain, but a different twist.

The main spiritual theme of this book deals with choices and the effects such decisions have upon others. The story revolves primarily around two families and how the choice of the parents—in this case fathers—affects their children. The Bible speaks in two ways about how parents influence their children and future generations. The first is to teach God's precepts to their children.

Deuteronomy 6:7
And you shall teach them diligently unto your children, and shall talk to them when you sit in your house, and when you walk by the way, and when you lie down, and when you rise up.

The second is more problematic.

Exodus 20:5-6
You shall not bow down yourself to them, nor serve them; for I, the Lord your God, am a jealous God, visiting the iniquity of the father upon the children unto the third and fourth generations of them that hate me; <u>and</u> showing mercy unto thousands of them that love me and keep my commandments.

Exodus 34:7
Keeping mercy for thousands, forgiving iniquity and transgression and sin, and who will by no means clear the guilty, visiting iniquity of the fathers upon the children and upon children's children.

14

I am in no way implying generational sin. No! Rather, how the sins of fathers have long-term effects the children will experience, not that children will be held accountable! The above Scriptures show God is merciful towards thousands who repent, but that doesn't mean the effects of sin are halted. There are consequences to all sin and unrighteousness on the corporate level as well as the personal. Even today, we Christians experience the ravages of sin and its effects on society's attitudes, morals and values as the Cup of Iniquity is filling. It touches and pollutes everything, but we remain pure before God in the personal sense due to our position in Christ.

The first family is Hugh's, brother of Marcellus, who fought to protect his four children in Book 1. He received mercy from Ellis for his actions. However, the choice he made back then produces challenges for he and his two eldest sons, 16-year-old Wess, and 14-year-old Bosely when they become caught up in the insurrection. The boys and their sisters were rescued from Ravendale by Avatar in Book 1, but were four years younger at the time.

The second family is Owain's, the Lord of Midessex and Member of the Council of Twelve. Owain was coerced by Marcellus to try to capture Ellis in Book 1. He repented and also received mercy from Ellis, but sentenced to a 4-year probation to regain his position. This story begins shortly after Owain has completed his sentence and again sits on the Council. Through his wife, Lanay, and eldest daughter, 17-year-old Gwen, the effects of Owain's past and present choices will be seen.

Wess, Bosely and Gwen play key roles in showing the consequences and contrast of the principle. Mercy is a secondary theme in how people respond when it is received.

❦

The Characters in Book 2
Central to the Theme

ELLIS faces the first serious challenge of his reign. He is now age 22, and his wisdom and determination will be tested. The choices he makes could have personal tragic consequences and a profound effect upon his kingdom. He is also a new father and this plays into his response to Hugh, Owain and their children. Questions regarding mercy, forgiveness and justice are easily used with describing Ellis' actions and reactions in the story.

MUSETTA was Latham's mistress and takes his place as the villain with access to the talisman and renegade Shadow Warriors, so she is self-explanatory.

HUGH is a diligent father who loves his children and wants the best for them. Thus he is the illustration of Deuteronomy 6:7. However when trouble comes, he is powerless to help his children. This is where his teaching and example will be tested in Wess and Bosley, who must make choices based upon what they know without his input or guidance.

WESS is the serious-minded, older brother, who models himself after his Uncle Iain, his mother's brother, and army general. Wess has a strong drive to protect since he remembers well what happened to his family at the hands of his other uncle—Marcellus. He fights bitterness and resentment in response to his family's ruthless past. The insurrection challenges his belief and directs his choice of what path he will take: repeat the past or break from its hold like his father.

BOSLEY is the more sensitive of the brothers and deeply impacted by their mother's death. As a result, he withdrew and his maturity retarded. Even at age 14, he stubbornly refuses to move beyond the past. It is when fleeing the insurrection that Bosley must grow up and face life and the harsh reality of the past he avoided.

OWAIN is the marked contrast of Hugh. His character flaws and weak personality once again lead to his bad decisions. He is an example of Exodus 20:5-6 and 34:7, of how his past action with Marcellus, and his present choice to join Musetta, will impact his family and Allon.

LANAY portrays the hapless wife. Hapless in the sense she suffers from a weakness in personality like Owain, and is paralyzed with fear into inaction. This fear keeps her from stopping Owain, either directly or telling someone else of his intent. Yes, wives should support their husband, but when direct sin is involved, she could act in his best interest and the protection of her daughters. The topic of fear is a good one in reference to Lanay. *For God has not given us a spirit of fear.* (2 Timothy 1:7), but we know where fear comes from. Sin of inaction is also as damaging as sin of action—omission and commission.

GWEN typifies stubbornness and rebellion. She is stronger in character than either Lanay or Owain, and uses that trait to dominate her mother. Many Biblical themes can be addressed with Gwen such as rebellion, submission to parents, honoring parents and outright rejection of Truth due to pride.

As I said earlier, I make clear and distinct divisions between Wess, Bosley and Gwen.

Suggested Questions
Allon - Book 2
(Feel free to make your own questions.)

1) Contrast and compare the way Owain and Hugh individually reacted to Ellis' mercy.
2) How does this show the ways in which people respond to God's mercy?
3) What troubled Hugh the most about Ellis' mercy and how did he react to Mahon?
4) What motivates Wess into action?
5) What made Bosley change his mind on the journey, and what was the result?
6) Contrast and compare Wess and Bosely's character. Whom do you identify with and why? Do you see areas God might want you to work on?
7) How do Wess and Bosley relate to their father? To their late mother? How do you relate to your parents?
8) What influenced Owain to make his decision to join Musetta? Do you let the opinions of others affect your behavior?
9) How did Lanay respond to Owain's behavior and insurrection? Could she have acted differently?
10) Describe Gwen. How is she different from Wess and Bosley?
11) Compare and contrast each family's choice in response to Ellis' decision. Where do you see Jor'el (God) at work in the judgments rendered?
12) What impact does all this have upon Ellis as a king and father?

Allon

Book 3

Heir Apparent

Shawn Lamb

Allon Books

Book 3 - Overview

THIS IS PERHAPS ONE OF THE MORE PERSONAL BOOKS of the series, as it focuses primarily on 16-year-old Nigel, Ellis' oldest child and heir. The story portrays how he interacts with his family. Thus, this story is more character-driven than by events. The theme is about *compromise*—or in most Bible translations—*steadfastness*. The Old Testament is filled with warnings from God about not compromising with different cultures or beliefs and remaining pure in thought and heart toward His principles and precepts.

Psalms 78: 7-8

That they might set their hope in God, and not forget the works of God, but keep His commandments; and might not be as their fathers, a stubborn and rebellious generations, a generation that set not their hearts right, and whose spirit was not <u>steadfast</u> with God.

There are numerous illustrations of what happened to Israel, or individuals who ignored God's warning and sinned against Him. The Babylonian captivity and all the compromises and punishments spoken of in Judges are just a few examples.

Verses also speak of blessings to those who keep God's statutes.

Psalms 1:2-3

But his delight is in the law of the Lord, and in His law does he meditate day and night. And he shall be like a tree planted by the rivers of water that brings forth fruit in its season, its leaf also shall not wither; and whatsoever he does shall prosper.

20

The test comes for Ellis and Nigel in a visit from a defeated enemy offering a marriage among the terms of peace treaty and homage for Ellis' victory. Diplomatically, Ellis can't outright refuse and risk another war, but Nigel grapples with the offer and his father's willingness to listen to the proposal. This sets the stage for what is to come.

While Ellis attempts to navigate delicate negotiations, Nigel becomes increasingly frustrated and worried about his future, but feels unable to speak honestly to his father about his concerns. Avatar, Nigel's Guardian Overseer, gives advice to his charge, but, like most teenage boys, Nigel lets his confusion and emotions rule rather than logic. Thus, father and son are in a state of avoidance on the heart of the issue: compromise or refusal.

Through family relationships and dynamics, various aspects of compromise, honesty, faith, trust and communication are explored. Grief is also a topic to deal with, both for the characters and for teaching when Nigel is killed.

The Characters in Book 2
Central to the Theme

ELLIS, at this point, is a rather indulgent father to Nigel and his three daughters, Ellan (15), Tristine (12) and Necie (10). Yes, he is stern with instruction of duty and learning, but toward their behavior he is toleratent. This can have both good and bad outcomes depending upon the situation, but in all, he love his children.

When the Morvenians arrive with the proposal, he must reconcile his decision both as king and father, not often an easy choice. In this area, father and son are very much alike and it causes friction in dealing with issues. Ellis hopes Nigel can understand his position; but it may be too much to ask of his son. Thus he grapples on how to handle the situation with the best outcome for his family and kingdom. A drastic shift in his perspective happens when Nigel is killed in a hunting accident. Bereft of his son, his focus turns to Ellan and will alter all relationships within the family.

NIGEL is suddenly hit with the first true test of his young adulthood; the prospect of marriage and his future reign as King of Allon. He is unsure how to handle his doubts and the nightmares that assail him. His one glaring weakness is his tendency to withdraw when it comes to confrontation with those he cares about. He vacillates about Avatar's counsel concerning faith and trust. His unwillingness to speak candidly to his father for fear of hurting him causes unnecessary tension and problems.

SHANNAN attempts to be the voice of reason and questions Ellis in his process of dealing with the situation. However, she doesn't speak to Nigel, a decision she will later regret.

AVATAR tries to use his position to offer Nigel wisdom and advice. However, being a Guardian, it is often difficult trying to tackle mortal emotional and relationship issues. He can't force Nigel to act or interfere in negotiations, only advise him. He is devastated when he is unable to save Nigel. He keenly feels he failed.

Through Avatar, Kell, Armus, Mahon, Morell and other Guardians I attempt to show a glimpse into angelic views of mortals in accordance with Scripture: their love for us, delivering of heavenly messages, willingness to protect and, perhaps, their disappointment and frustration when we make wrong decisions.

ELLAN can be fastidious and overbearing at times in her desire to relate to Nigel and Ellis. In her own way she seeks approval, yet exhibits intolerance and jealousy toward Tristine and her relationship to their father and brother. Ellan and Tristine are totally different in personality and clash almost daily. In this relationship, Ellis' fault of indulgence is seen and will later reap harsh consequences when the family dynamics are forever changed by Nigel's death.

At first Ellan is stunned to hear about Nigel, but overwhelmed at suddenly becoming heir to the throne. With Morrell's help, she steels herself for the task and newfound determination to use her position to correct what she believes is both Nigel and Ellis' weakness—taming Tristine.

TRISTINE – As the middle child, she benefits from more freedom than either Nigel or Ellan, and takes advantage. However, she loves Nigel dearly and mimics him in everything. In turn, Nigel favors her, which is a source of contention among the siblings. Tristine also loves her parents and thrives on Ellis' pride in her accomplishments, further provoking Ellan.

Tristine deeply feels the impact of Nigel's death. He was her beloved brother, shield against the world and most vocal supporter. Vulnerable and hurt, she must find a way to cope and face the future without him.

DARIUS tries to act as mediator between Ellis and the Morvenians. As *uncle*, he intervenes at points in the story with Nigel and Tristine. Like Shannan, he serves as a voice of reason.

There are others in the story serving to illustrate the point of compromise or remaining steadfast. In each of the main characters, faith is tested and/or shaken in the face of possible compromise for peace and death.

Suggested Questions
Allon - Book 3

(Feel free to make your own questions.)

1. To whom was the marriage proposal originally made?
2. Why was Nigel disturbed when he became the focus of the marriage proposal?
3. How would the marriage compromise Nigel and Ellis' beliefs? Are you ever asked to compromise your beliefs? (2 Tim. 1:12-13)
4. Describe Nigel's nightmare? From whom was he running and why?
5. What reason does Nigel give for not speaking to his father? Is that right? Do you ever fear talking to your parents? If so, why or why not? (2 Tim. 1:7 & Deut. 5:16)
6. Compare Nigel's relationship to Ellan and then to Tristine. Did he treat them fairly? How do you treat your siblings?
7. What makes Ellan jealous of Tristine? How does she use that jealousy against Tristine?
8. Who do Ellis and Nigel meet on their journey to go hunting?
9. How does Ellis response to Nigel's attempt to discuss the matter? What is the end result? How could that have been avoided? (Ephesians 4:26b)
10. Discuss the impact of Nigel's death on each family member. How does Ellis react? Ellan? Tristine? What similarities or differences do you see?

Allon

Book 4

A Question

of
Sovereignty

Shawn Lamb

Allon Books

Book 4 - Overview

THIS BOOK BRINGS BACK A MORE EPIC FEEL, but is driven by a family in crisis. Five years have passed since the events in *Heir Apparent* and much has changed in the royal family.

In this story, I pattern Ellis after King David and the problems David had as a result of his ineptness as a father and Godly example to his children. Ellis isn't as bad a father as David, but his indulgence has been replaced by frustration, intolerance and urgency in preparing Ellan for her role as future queen and finding her a suitable husband. As a result, his actions, and sometimes inaction, cause rifts, confrontations, bitterness and jealousy to thrive, and opens the door for a long-time enemy to work right under his nose.

The strained relationship between Ellan and Tristine has turned into a spiteful rivalry. It reaches a critical point when Sullivan and his mother, Musetta (both disguised as Gorham royalty) arrive at Waldron. They give Ellan the avenue to vent her spleen on Tristine and manipulate Ellis. It also reveals Morrell's true mission and his responsibility in killing Nigel, not a hunting accident as is believed, but an assassination.

The dark machinations of Musetta and Sullivan for complete revenge are made easier by the dismal state of the royal family. The whole fate of Allon hinges upon the king who follows Ellis—the Great King as foretold in Prophecy. With Nigel's death, it will not be a son of royal blood, which leads to the question of who?

Tristine becomes pivotal to the story in her efforts to withstand Musetta and Sullivan and somehow jar Ellis out of his spiritual slumber to see what is happening to his family before it is too late. As such, she becomes the focus of the enemy to drive a wedge between them. She is sent fleeing, and on her journey, meets two unlikely allies: a wandering crippled name Waymon, and Tyrone, a blacksmith. Both are more than they appear.

This story is tough and hard, with themes of faith, neglect, testing, failure, perseverance and loss being explored. I pull no punches about sin and the consequences, both with Ellis and Ellan. Like David with Absalom, Ellis' failure in protecting and nurturing his family will cost him dearly. Ellis and his family are examples of how easily people can fall into temptations and sin when not diligent in guarding their hearts and minds.

The Characters in Book 4 Central to the Theme

ELLIS – Since Nigel's death, Ellis has allowed his sense of urgency and own effort to fulfill prophecy about the Great King to dominate his actions. He is so consumed that he fails to see many problems arising from his myopic objective. All relationships hang by a thread. Shannan and Darius attempt to help him correct matters before it is too late, but their efforts are interrupted by the arrival of Sullivan and Musetta.

With craft and subtly, mother and son work their wiles to further drive a wedge between family members, and even affect the Guardians. The playing field was ripe for their arrival.

DARIUS – Confrontation after confrontation with Ellis over Musetta and Sullivan leads him to take matters into his own hands. He dispatchs a messenger to Gorhman to learn the truth. But discovering Musetta's identity leads to his death. Yet, some good comes of it, as the loss of Darius begins to awaken Ellis to the truth of what is happening.

SHANNAN – This is one time her efforts to corral and influence Ellis will be thwarted by his stubbornness and the aid Morrell lends to Musetta and Sullivan. Although she is sent from Waldron due to a scheme to separate her and Ellis, Shannan devises a plan to return and stop them, even when it means sacrificing her own life. Her death is the most heart-wrenching consequence Ellis will face.

TRISTINE – Compelled by a sense of danger and evil to resist Musetta and Sullivan, she bitterly clashes with Ellis and Ellan. Eventually, Morrell acts and Tristine flees Waldron. Driven by love for Ellis and fear concerning the fate of Allon, she will join forces with Tyrone, Kell and Armus to stop Musetta, Sullivan and Morrell. Like her mother and Darius, Tristine is the example of a believer who will resist evil and defend God no matter the cost. It is by her faithfulness, courage and loyalty, her prayer is heard and Ellis is healed.

ELLAN is the example of an unregenerate person. Even growing up in a home where Jor'el (God) is honored, she never embraces him, rather rejects him for pride's sake. Seeds were planted in Book 3 and began to blossom after Nigel's death. Yes, Ellis provoked her by some of his actions and demands, but in the end Ellan makes her own choice to rebel and join Musetta, Sullivan and Morrell to destroy her family.

SULLIVAN is the wolf in sheep's clothing. His only purpose is to tear apart that which is joined together. Being Latham's son, he is another example of those who are children of the devil, the father of lies and prince of this world. They can beguile and entice, but their end is destruction.

TYRONE, being half-mortal, half-Guardian, is a picture of Christ, as he suffers persecution and social rejection for who he is. Through faith in Jor'el, his nature and character shows mercy, compassion and strength. When Tristine comes along, he is prepared to leave his isolation for the unknown – which turns out that he is the Great King of Prophecy. He is the one who conquers the Dark Way, not Ellis, who forfeited his right to rule by his actions.

WAYMON (Nigel) – Yes, Nigel is alive, only made a cripple by Morrell's assassination attempt on the hunting trip in Book 3. However, the early fear that kept him from speaking to Ellis about the marriage, also kept him from telling his family he was alive. Gripped by shame and guilt, he chooses to wander Allon as a nameless, crippled beggar. Only the threat to his family spurs him to action, but even then only sporadically. In a desperate move, he attempts to save his mother but fails. He does intervene in protecting Tristine and is reunited with his family.

Nigel comes full circle, and only after he releases his bitterness and regret to accept what happened to him, can he receive mercy and healing. He is the believer restored after years of struggle.

Suggested Questions
Allon - Book 4

(Feel free to make your own questions.)

1. Why is Ellis so intent on finding Ellan a husband?
2. Describe the differences in the relationship between Ellan and Tristine from Book 3 to Book 4. Do you see much of a change? Why or Why not?
3. Who is Sullivan's father?
4. How are Sullivan and Musetta able to mask their identities from the Guardians while at Waldron?
5. What was the cause of Darius' sudden illness?
6. Why did Tristine leave Waldron the first time? Who does she meet on her journey?
7. Describe Tyrone and Waymon. How are they alike? And how are they different?
8. What discovery does Armus make after being wounded by Shadow Warriors in his search for Tristine?
9. How does the rift among the mortals affect the Guardians?
10. When Tristine returns what did Ellis say her running away caused? How do Kell and Avatar react?
11. Who killed Darius?
12. When Tristine, Tyrone, Kell and Armus are united, whom do they encounter? And what is the result?
13. Why does Nigel refuse to tell his family he is alive?
14. Who poisoned Ellis? Why?
15. Why do Ellan and Sullivan hold a tournament?
16. Who defeats Sullivan? How does this impact Ellan and Musetta?
17. How does Ellis deal with the horrible consequences of his actions?
18. What happens to Nigel?

Allon

Book 5

Gauntlet

Shawn Lamb

Allon Books

Book 5 - Overview

GAUNTLET BEGINS A RUN OF 3 BOOKS THAT VENTURE outside of Allon, brining into play other cultures, myths and religions. Each will deal with personal issues, interacting with non-believers and the rewards of succeeding or the consequences of sin and/or failure.

The major spiritual themes in *Gauntlet* are redemption and restoration with the two primary examples being Nigel and Mirit. Through Nigel, the topics of testing and temptation are also explored. Mirit is the pivotal figure in showing irresistible grace or divine election. Whichever term one wishes to use, there is no denying God draws people to Him in an act of gracious salvation.

John 6:44
No man can come to me except the Father, which has sent me, draw him.

This is the Greek word *heiko*, meaning to literally drag and bring together. Jesus uses the same word in describing the effects of his crucifixion.

John 12:32
*And I, being lifted up from the earth, will **draw** all men unto me.*

There is also –

Romans 8:29
For whom He did foreknow, he also did predestinate to be conformed to the image of His Son.

But this not a treatise on predestination or elect rather an explanation of my use of allegory to illustrate the calling of a believer.

Characters from Allon and Tunlund will provide various glimpses on how people respond when faced with direct challenges and assaults on their personal beliefs. I do not sugarcoat sin or attempt to downplay the effects and consequences of bad choices, but neither do I cross the line in any portrayal.

The Characters in Book 5 Central to the Theme

Titus – Although only 7 years old, during his kidnapping and the harrowing circumstances, he displays a great deal of faith and trust in Jor'el, his Uncle Nigel and his father – Tyrone. He is the example Christ repeatedly gives regarding children and child-like faith.

Matthew 19:14
Permit little children, and forbid them not, to come unto me, for of such is the kingdom of heaven.

Mark 10:15
Verily I say unto you, whosoever shall not receive the kingdom of God as a little child, he shall not enter.

Tyrone is the believer who must overcome prejudice and scheming. The scorn for his low half-breed birth followed him from his isolation to the throne of Allon. Like those who did not believe a simple carpenter from Nazareth could be the Messiah, many cannot accept Tyrone as the Great King, and he must confront their evil machinations and attempts to destroy him. His struggle and confrontation at the ruins in Tunlund is his Gethsemane.

Nigel – During the covert mission to rescue Titus, he faces his first test of strength and courage as the Jor'ellian Knight of Temple and the King's Champion. All his training and beliefs will be challenged in Tunlund. He is the example of how the believer must keep the armor in good condition at all times and be ready to expertly handle the sword, the most powerful offensive and defensive weapon.

When he meets Mirit, the testing becomes more personal than he expects. Interaction with her brings up memories of his past days as a wandering cripple, of his cynicism and dealing with his own restoration and second chance. He must also learn to forgive and show mercy when the situation takes a dramatic turn and he learns the truth about Mirit.

MIRIT is perhaps the most pivotal character of the whole book and serves as the focus of redemption and restoration. Although she lacks memory of her life due to an accident, she never seeks to discover her past, never attempts to learn what life was like before. In fact, she becomes comfortable in her surrounds. Most non-believers go blissfully along in their lives until something comes along to shake things up—God. Whether He uses people or circumstances, He seeks to get their attention to *draw* them to Him. In this case, Nigel serves as the catalyst for Mirit.

Despite their constant clashes, she recognizes Nigel is different and slowly comes to appreciate why. This appreciation brings to the surface underlying issues Mirit wasn't aware existed. Inexplicably she can speak a language, circumstances compel to change her course and life, and even when she doesn't understand why - she is willing to trust Jor'el to help her rectify what she did.

Mirit's death and her subsequent reviving serve as a dramatic picture of a person dying to the old man and becoming a new fully restored creature in Christ. Like all new believers, she must adjust and grow, but the act is one time and forever.

NADIA is the true believer of another religion, a fanatic. She is Nigel's strongest opposition and poses the greatest danger to the mission. Time and again, she shows she is willing to go to any lengths to server her false god.

DANTE and Nadia are cut from the same fanatical cloth. Only Dante is so deceived, he truly believes he can be immortal. This adds a dimension of madness to his character that drives the entire story in his effort to gain immortality. Even at the end, he finds it unbelievable that he could die.

LANZO is the example of Judas. Under the guise of being an ambassador, he uses his crafty, diplomatic skills to deceive Tyrone and Nigel. Once unmasked, he seeks to kill and scorns those who once considered him an ally.

LUKAS – In a lesser way than Mirit, he shows the positive side of a wayward person accepting God. He also serves as an example of God's divine plan and how He interacts in the lives of all men. Lukas was compelled to save Mirit's life after his pirate raid. He sheltered her, raised her and came to love her as his own child.

TAMAR serves a twofold purpose, first in tempting Nigel and challenging his faith and commitment to Jor'el and personal purity. Later she is seen as an example of one seeking and finding mercy for her sins.

LORAN is the prime example of how bile begets bile. As Gareth's son, he spent a lifetime bombarded by scorn, enmity and bitterness. Only he takes it a step further than his father or his uncle, Zebulon, by willingly aiding the enemy in an attempt to topple Tyrone and destroy Allon. He is an example of someone controlled by hate and a hardened heart that nothing can penetrate. He knows no love, mercy or compassion.

ULLOCK is the unregenerate man ruled by his lusts; whether lust for war, power or women. He makes no attempt at self-control.

STAMOS typifies the fence-sitter; the person who tries to remain neutral, but all his efforts are for nothing, and he becomes victimized by his own lack of moral stance. He failed to honor his late wife's wishes to keep Tamar pure. He allows Nadia to ruin his family and bring his tribe to the brink of destruction. Although he recognizes his fault, he doesn't seek forgiveness or attempt to make restitution rather lets Jaeger and the elders deal with the consequences.

Suggested Questions
Allon - Book 5

(Feel free to make your own questions.)

1. In what ways does Mirit remind Nigel of his past? How are they similar? How are they different?
2. How does Nigel react to the Tunlundian's religion and customs? Why? Are all religions created equal?
3. What caused Avatar to lose his strength and power?
4. How does Nigel react to learning of Mirit's involvement in Titus' kidnapping?
5. What sign did Lukas ask for to know if Jor'el existed? Do you ever ask God for a sign? Why?
6. How is Titus an example of faith?
7. What was Hueil's purpose in drawing Tyrone to the ruins?
8. How does Tyrone overcome Hueil? What does Scripture say about resisting the devil?
9. Name those who sought forgiveness and those who didn't. Give reasons.
10. What was Vidar's mission? What was the outcome?
11. What motivated Loran to act?
12. Describe Nigel and Mirit's relationship at the beginning, in the middle and at the end. What led to the changes?

Allon

Book 6

Dilemma

Shawn Lamb

Allon Books

Book 6 - Overview

THE MAIN THEME OF DILEMMA IS **CONTENTMENT.** Scripture uses words for contentment 37 times in both the Old and New Testament. The Hebrew word is *Ya'al*, which means an *act of volition, willing, give assent.* Several verses in Judges and 1 & 2 Kings add to this *willingness of action* by placing the word *be* in front of *content.* Even in Hebrew, the word for *be* is an action verb, such as found in

Psalms 46:10
Be still and know that I am God.

In the New Testament, the Greek root shows a different side of the same attitude with *Arkeo,* meaning to *raise a barrier, to keep in mind, to be satisfied.* The idea of a barrier is a form of protection in defense against the worldly lust assaulting the knowledge of God's provision.

Jesus tells soldiers in **Luke 3:14**
"… be content with your wages."

In **Philippians 4:11**, Paul says,
"I have learned, in whatever state I am, in this to be content."

Perhaps the most comprehensive verse is **Hebrews 13:5**
Let your manner of life be without covetousness, and be content with such things as you have; for He has said, I will never leave you, nor forsake you.

Contentment is a choice of action to stand upon God's word and faithfulness, and not a feeling during any given situation.

When all forms of lust act as a temptation against contentment, the origin of lust is *Pride*. This is the secondary theme of *Dilemma*.

There are 49 verses dealing with *pride* in Scripture. Perhaps the most famous Biblical quote is known almost worldwide:

Proverbs 16:18
Pride goes before destruction, and a haughty spirit before a fall.

Two main Hebrew words are used and are translated as either *haughty* or *arrogance*. The definition of both is *raised up in importance* and *puffed up in heart*, denoting the opposite of both *Ya'al* and *Arkeo* by choosing to give assent to raise self over God. All the verses dealing with pride and haughtiness/arrogance always result in destructive behavior, actions or consequences and divine judgment.

The Characters in Book 6 Central to the Theme

Auriel – As a Guardian, Auriel holds a privileged position in serving both mortals and Jor'el (God). Being a warrior, she is among the strongest caste of Guardians. In the position of Trio Leader, she shoulders great responsibility for the welfare of the mortals in the South Plains. However, centuries of festering anger and bitterness become unleashed, first upon Avatar, then against all her fellow Guardians when she betrays them and joins Shadow Warriors to invade Allon.

However, it is not until challenged by Skule that she admits to herself the strongest motivation is pride; pride of being a mighty warrior and seeking acknowledgement, and nothing anyone did or didn't do that caused her to act.

Skule – His cleverness joined with his dark power as a Shadow Warrior deceives everyone around him, including his compatriots. He is a master of the art of manipulation because he understands and accepts the reality of *pride*. He embraced it and *pride* became his greatest weapon. He represents the deceptiveness of Satan when appealing to an individual's *pride*. Though it doesn't take much to coax humans seeing as the *heart is deceitful above all things*. (Jeremiah 17:9) How Satan convinced other angels to follow him is a mystery.

Virgil – Although a Guardian, by way of Virgil I show confusion that can come to believers when under duress. Some deal with a helpless and trapped feeling, yet when tested, the true heart is revealed and regained. Character and resolve are forged with pressure.

CHAD is an example of a believer who decides to listen to his lustful heart over the 9 years of instruction and Godly behavior modeled by Nigel. I use him to boldly and poignantly demonstrate how sin and selfish actions can result in devastating consequences. By the end of the book, his pride is broken and his spirit in agony. I used the way Nigel, Mirit and Avatar reaction to Chad to show the unmerited grace, forgiveness, mercy and restoration granted when true repentance is reached.

BERGETA is a true believer in her false religious system. Even in the face of overwhelming danger and confronted with the truth, she clings to her powerless faith by making a declaration against Jor'el (God).

Although caught up in the situation due to association with Chad, her choice is a factor in her ultimate fate. This must be understood: each human has free will to make a choice when faced with Truth about God. He doesn't punish on a whim. His justice is righteous all together and justified by His willingness to grant mercy and salvation to those who call upon Him. Bergeta had her chance onboard ship to accept Jor'el and rejected it. As difficult as this concept is for some to accept, since we want to box God into our system of perceived justice, it is reality.

FARREN, WILDA and **KEARA** are used as examples of discontentment and pride. **FARREN'S** jealousy of Avatar propels her, along with her lust for a mortal. Even when confronted by Auriel about her past, she casts blame on others, another sign of *pride* —the inability to accept fault.

WILDA caves to peer pressure and follows her Trio Mates into betrayal and exile. **KEARA** gives into fear, a powerful emotion that can lead to serious ramifications.

45

Other **GUARDIANS** exhibit various forms of discord between male and female. I chose to use the Guardians since they are supposed to reflect harmony and heavenly attitudes. Mortals already experience the battle of the sexes so that is a clichéd theme.

The origin of this conflict harkens back to Genesis 3:16 where God curses the woman and says,

> *"… your desire shall be to your husband, and he shall rule over you."*

The same word for *desire* is also used in Genesis 4:7 where God is speaking to Cain about his offering.

> *"… sin lies at the door, and you shall be his desire, and shall rule over him."*

This isn't talking about physical desire, as some wrongly suggest, rather the word means *to dominate, to control, to usurp.* What woman hasn't chafed under authority, and *desired* to prove herself equal to or better than a man? Now, this isn't a dissertation about submission, rather an explanation of where the discord is rooted.

The act of working together is for the mutual benefit of all and in harmony with the order established by God. Thus to show that strength of males is a futile thing and how women are valued in relationships, Jor'el (God) dictates how the battle will happen—not in might, rather in obedience to Him. This is the key to all relationships: obedience and submission to God; and why in *Dilemma*, I attempt to show everything must come under the obedience and submission to Jor'el (God). If it doesn't, the consequences can be fatal.

Suggested Questions
Allon - Book 6

(Feel free to make your own questions.)

1. Why does Auriel say she is angry at Avatar? How does she act out her anger? Have you ever held unspoken anger toward anyone?
2. Why did Farren leave Allon?
3. How is the authority in Soren unbiblical?
4. What is the biblical model for authority? Can you name verses to support your answer?
5. What made Chad discontent? Have you felt discontent? Why? How did you deal with those feelings?
6. How does Chad's view of Guardians differ from Nigel?
7. Does Chad's sin affect Nigel, Mirit and Avatar? Why?
8. What about Bergeta? Did she influence Chad? How does her actions affect her father and the mission?
9. What happens to Bergeta? Why?
10. Does this help you to see how a single person's sin can harm others?
11. What effect – if any – did Skule have on Auriel's decision? What word did he use to describe her betrayal?
12. How did the worshipful attention influence Auriel's choice?
13. In what ways did these characters show discontentment and/or pride? Auriel. Farren. Chad.
14. Why was Virgil restored to warrior status?

Allon

Book 7

Dangerous Deception

Shawn Lamb

Allon Books

BOOK 7 - OVERVIEW

T HE MAIN THEMES AND PRINCIPLES OF THIS BOOK ARE rebellion, jealousy and pride. However, it is *pride* from which rebellion and jealousy emerge. Based upon the translation, the word *pride* appears 49 times in the King James Version and 69 times in the New International Version. This is due to the various meanings and derivatives of the Greek and Hebrew words.

Three primary Hebrew words are used in the Old Testament; though many derivatives appear in other verses, these are the main examples.

- In Leviticus 26:19 *"I will break the pride of your power"* is the Hebrew word *gaown,* which can mean *majesty or excellency.*
- In 1 Samuel 17:28 when David is accosted by his eldest brother for scolding the men of Israel for fleeing the Philistines, the word *zadown* is used for *pride* and means *presumption* or *arrogance.*
- In Psalms 31:20, David voices confidence in God's protection of the righteous when he says, *"You shall hide them in the secret of your presence from the pride of man."* Here the word *rokec* is used, which means *pride,* yet comes for the root meaning a *snare.*

In the New Testament, three Greek words are used for *pride.* The first is *huperphania,* which means *haughtiness, proud, appearing above others.* It is found in Mark 7:22 where Jesus gives a list of the evils that proceed from the heart and includes *pride.*

The second is *tuphoo,* which in literal translations means *smoke or puffed up;* we say *high-minded.* This is found in 1 Timothy 3:6 when

49

Paul is describing the qualifications of a deacon, *"not a novice, lest being lifted up with pride he falls into the condemnation of the devil."*

The final Greek word is *alazoneia,* which comes from the root *alazon,* meaning *braggadocios* or *full of boasting pride.* It is used by John in one of the most quoted New Testament verses:

1 John 2:16
"For all that is in the word, the lust of the flesh, and the lust of the eyes, and the pride of life, is not of the Father, but is of the world."

Some of the harshest verses and displays of God's judgment occur in the Old Testament and are associated with *rebellion.* God constantly punished Israel for continuous rebellion, with the most significant times being the Babylonian captivity, enslavement in Egypt and 40 years of wandering in the wilderness. God brings this down to the parental level with instructions to use strong discipline to curb the natural sinful tendency of children to rebel. The parallels between how God treated the *children* of Israel should be clearly seen in His divine parental instruction.

Only one word is used in the Old Testament to describe *jealousy,* the Hebrew word *qana.* This denotes a purposeful action or choice to *stir up envy* or *to provoke.* The singular word in the New Testament is *zelos,* where we get the word *zealous* or *zeal.* Again, it is to *provoke a feeling against* or *create a fervent mind against.* In both Testaments, these words speak about actions taken *to provoke the Lord to jealousy* or give warning against taking such action to *stir up God's wrath.*

The primary characters used to exemplify these principles are Titus, Tyrone and Nigel. Although in Nigel's case, he is more the object than causing or instigating the feelings, but figures into the results.

With the accursed Guardians, Onedo and Raiden, I attempt to show the emotions that drove Lucifer to act—pride, jealous and rebellion—and the curse pronounced upon him and those who followed. (Isaiah 14:12-20) By way of Ridge, Egan and Avatar, I try to visualize the effect on those who remain faithful. One can only imagine how heavenly angels responded when given the choice to remain faithful or follow Lucifer, as Scripture is silent. But the end result is the heavenly angels must battle against those of their fellow servants who turned. Their fate is sealed.

The Characters in Book 7 Central to the Theme

TITUS, now twelve years old, has let the experiences of Tunlund (Book 5) when he was only 7 influence him in a wrong direction. The gratitude he felt for Nigel rescuing him has turned to an unhealthy exaltation, even to the point of shunning his father, King Tyrone, in all aspects of his life. Along with the elevated admiration, Titus has become puffed-up by enduring and surviving the Tunlund ordeal. Combined, these feelings grow to the point of planning a bold act of defiance by stowing away on the ship to Natan.

When caught, Titus displays no remorse, regret or comprehension of how his *pride* and action affects others. Even being locked in the brig and accused of *rebellion* doesn't curb his attitude. Not until the situation in Natan becomes desperate and deadly, does Titus begin to acknowledge his wrongdoing. The peril is especially driven home when watching Tyrone face the Natanese warrior in deadly combat then witnessing Allard's death. Pride becomes replaced by deep-seeded guilt. Overcoming trauma to admit his fault is a difficult yet necessary step in healing the hurt and pain he caused.

TYRONE – Although he possesses a heavenly side to his character and nature, Tyrone succumbs to the most base of mortal emotion: *jealousy*. In his heart, he knows better where Nigel is concerned, but after continually being provoked to anger by Titus, his wounded *pride* imagines all sorts of malice against Nigel, thus rousing *jealousy*.

Blinded by emotions he has yet to admit, Tyrone goes after Titus. By assuming the identity of a royal officer, Tyrone is in essence doing what he accused Nigel: making an excuse. Even when confronted by Tristine, he refuses to see the parallel. Like his son, Tyrone's realization occurs during confrontations in Natan. Unlike his son, he understands the dangers facing the group and, despite his wounded pride, exemplifies the necessity of submission for the good of others. He is a king becoming a servant. Through his actions, Titus comes to view him in a different light, one of unselfish caring to the point of sacrifice.

NIGEL – In a long overdue conversation with Mirit, he finally deals with the painful past of his crippling. (Books 3 & 4) This will play a key role when it comes to confronting Titus, both onboard ship and later during their escape. Although tenderhearted towards his family, in this case, Nigel is the *object* rather than the *cause* of Titus and Tyrone's actions. Still, he must deal with correcting his nephew's rebellious behavior while protecting Tyrone in their role-playing. Tyrone's jealousy was unknown to him, as told by his reaction to the confession. Nigel only knew the friction between them was due to Titus.

Regardless of the pride, anger, jealousy and rebellion directed at him, Nigel doesn't react in kind rather continues to look out for the welfare of others. He takes his role of First Jor'ellian and the King's Champion to heart when shielding Tyrone from discovery and then confronting Titus for complicating his duty of protecting the king! Nigel exemplifies how Christians are to respond with *agape* love, always thinking of the welfare of others no matter the circumstances.

ALLARD represents the elder imparting wisdom to the younger during his dialogues with Titus. Being an objective party, Allard can speak to Titus in ways the boy would reject from Tyrone or Nigel. When wounded, he becomes the focal point of Titus' interest; an interest brought about by guilt, yet necessary for understanding. His death serves as the biggest impact upon Titus. Although the fact that such would have happened without Titus' presence, it proves vital to the boy's turning.

CHAD – His involvement with Titus shows that *"All things work together for good ..."* (Romans 8:28). Chad's *rebellious* behavior in Soren (Book 6), uniquely qualifies him to challenge Titus. He also serves to bridge the gap between nephew and uncle when speaking to Nigel after Titus' discovery.

EGAN – Anger and jealousy aren't only mortal issues, and quickly rise to the surface when Egan comes face-to-face with Ridge. Memories of the past haunt him, stirring his anger while jealously protective of Titus. It hinders his duty and complicates his participation on the mission. Avatar's initial confrontation in Yuki does little to dissuade Egan. Although Titus questions him in regards to Ridge, passion drives him to the brink of oblivion. The encounter with Raiden completely disarms Egan with profound realization of his behavior, draining away centuries of anger and hostility.

RIDGE – Like Nigel, Ridge is the *object* of intense anger. True, he and Egan did not reach Lord Willis in time to save him, but Ridge is not responsible for the mortal's death. Despite Egan's continued threats and innuendos, Ridge does hold secret regret concerning Willis. Such feelings do not manifest in like action or attitude toward Egan; and he remains steadfast in his task and duty to Jor'el and the mortals. For him, the revelation is a relief of conscience.

AVATAR – This mighty warrior of the Elite Trio is stunned to the core when meeting Raiden. The vacancy of spirit in Raiden's eyes reflected a frightening reality of what Avatar avoided in Tunlund (Book 5) when he resisted Hueil.

His statement in the cave regarding Raiden can relate to all who reject God. Their so-called good works on earth will come to nothing for they have no eternal value. Scripture talks about the testing of works with burning of wood, hay and stumble, leaving only the gold, silver and precious stones. Avatar's choice to continue in his faithful service meant his life's work mattered. Oh, but what it could have been if he had chosen wrongly!

Suggested Questions
Allon - Book 7

(Feel free to make your own questions.)

1. Have you ever been jealous of someone? Why? How did you respond when confronted about your feelings?
2. What made Titus believe he could speak to the young Emperor? Have you ever felt you could do something you weren't prepared for?
3. Have you disobeyed your parents by being someplace or doing something you were told not to?
4. Has anyone gotten into trouble for helping you to disobey?
5. Describe the word *pride*.
6. How did Nigel react to Titus' rebellion?
7. What do you think would have happened if Titus obeyed his father? What wouldn't have happened?
8. How did the situation help those involved? Ridge? Egan? Titus? Tyrone?
9. Since the false gods are rebellious Guardians, who do you think the false gods are in our world? Can you find Scripture to help learn the answer?

Allon

Book 8

Divided

Shawn Lamb

Allon Books

Book 8 - Overview

DIVIDED TIES UP STORYLINES from *Book 4: A Question of Sovereignty* and *Book 5: Gauntlet*. Once again, the dynamics of family relationship are explored. Sometimes unresolved issues can fester and cause major problems. Other times, individual choices can have unintended and deadly consequences. Both of these situations involve taking personal responsibility and seeking forgiveness—or lack thereof.

A topic that is not often discussed in families is the fact that siblings can be treated the same by parents, experience identical rearing through punishment and instruction yet come away with different reactions. This can cause great parental angst and heartache when they feel they did their best before God. It also makes siblings very frustrated. However, why this occurs is not a mystery.

Jeremiah 17:9
The heart is deceitful about all things, and desperately wicked. Who can know it?

Even when parents follow Scripture to the letter in raising children, it is the responsibility of the child to follow, obey and, in the end, choose whether to embrace God or not. The vast disparity between Tristine and Ellan comes to a fever pitch in *Divided*, and reveals two opposite responses to their upbringing. Nigel serves as a third response, as he vacillates about bridging the gap.

Troubled family relationships are not solely relegated to the older siblings of King Ellis, but also mirrored in the children of Tyrone and Tristine. Family history can impact succeeding generations. (See

Allon – Book 2 – Insurrection Overview for further explanation of generational impact.) Titus and Fraser become examples of interaction with each other and reaction to their parents due to the situation involving their mother and her siblings. In the end, the brothers and Tyrone will reflect one of the most well known parables in Scripture - The Prodigal Son.

Another theme that involves choice is the topic of abuse. Is one a victim or a victor? How can such a situation impact the choice? Where can one go to gain the strength to overcome? This comes by way of Valery and her father, Braden.

Although everything might seem complex with the various families and their interactions, it really boils down to individual choices.

Joshua 24:15
"Choose you this day, whom you will serve ..."

The key to making any choice is the heart toward or against God. The Western culture uses the word *heart* to refer to feelings. However, in the Jewish mindset the terms used for *heart* means *behavior*, and are found over 800 times in Scripture. That is what the characters in *Divided* represent, different forms of the *heart* according to God's standard as outlined in the Bible.

The Characters in Book 8
Central to the Theme

ELLAN serves as an example of the hardened and unrepentant heart. Instead of rethinking her actions while in prison, she takes her alliance with the Dark Way further than before.

In *A Question of Sovereignty*, she let her selfishness dictate her actions by becoming involved with Musetta and Sullivan's plot against her father, King Ellis. In *Divided*, she willingly makes a pact with Hueil to give him what he wants in exchange for complete revenge against Tristine. Her choice goes beyond a personal vendetta, to realm of the eternal when she aligns with Hueil.

TRISTINE serves as an example of an obedient heart. Despite being rattled by Ellan's return, she understands that stepping aside is the only way to stop her vengeful sister. By this act of compliance, she can protect her children and defend her country.

NIGEL is an example of the mature heart. In *Divided,* his life comes full-circle in respect to his position in the family. Known for being tenderhearted and a pushover with some family members, Nigel has grown to understand his place and purpose. This realization is tested when he must accept the crown to defend one sister against another.

TYRONE again serves as an example of a submissive heart. Unlike in Natan, he faces severe tests when his entire family and kingdom is at stake! Normally indomitable in faith and trust, Tyrone's confidence in Nigel is sorely tested when Hueil plays with his mind by inducing visions. The resulting discovery of Fraser's stupidity drives Tyrone to the brink of doing the unthinkable!

When Tyrone finally regains his composure from the ordeal, he can welcome back Fraser with open arms. Tyrone acts the part of the overjoyed father in the parable of Prodigal Son, willing to receive his repentant son without question and shower him with love and grace.

FRASER is the foolish heart that becomes changed. In his mind, he knows what is right and expected of him. Yet he chafes under the delusion of his own intelligence and station. He becomes puffed-up and prideful. All these aspects combined, lead him to fall easily into Ellan and Hueil's trap.

Learning how his foolishness almost destroyed his family sends Fraser into a dismal state from which he sees no hope of escape or restoration. He becomes a bit of a wanderer, though not to the extent Nigel once did. In fact, Nigel's example serves as a catalyst for Fraser to even dare a return. Humiliated, ashamed and repentant, he doesn't expect forgiveness. The reaction of his father and warmth of family acceptance overwhelms him.

TITUS acts like the stubborn heart. Having learned a harsh lesson in Natan, Titus isn't too tolerant of Fraser's impulsive and reckless behavior. Although protective of Fraser because he is his brother, Titus is openly critical of Tyrone's handling of Fraser. In a few incidents, Titus represents the older brother in the parable of Prodigal Son. However, he isn't as stubborn as to turn his back on either his father or brother at the end.

ELLIS is the heart of a loyal friend who sticks closer than a brother. Ellis' father named him after the late King Ellis, who was a friend and benefactor of his family. He is Titus' closest friend, and future brother-in-law. Titus is betrothed to Ellis' younger sister.

In such a unique position, Ellis acts with Titus in a manner most would not dare in accosting the royal prince. Titus tends to take advantage of Ellis' friendship, like when asking the woman-shy, tongue-tied Ellis to shield him from Lady Valery. Ellis' compassionate personality and loyalty aid Valery in overcoming a lifetime of hidden abuse.

VALERY is the deeply wounded heart. Even when raised to believe and have faith in Jor'el, she safeguards herself from outsiders. Being combative toward Titus is a manifestation of being on the defensive. With Ellis, Valery slowly learns she doesn't have to be on guard all the time while her association with Mirit, helps her to gain the courage to face her battered past and find a way to move on.

Suggested Questions
Allon - Book 8
(Feel free to make your own questions.)

1. When Ellan told Fraser to write the fake letter, what did he do?
2. Have you ever been asked by someone to do something you knew was wrong? How did you respond?
3. Read Luke 15:11-32. Can you name this parable?
4. Who does Tyrone remind you of in the Luke 15 parable? Why?
5. What character in the parable does Fraser sound like? Why?
6. Have you ever had a problem forgiving someone?
7. How did Valery respond when faced with her father in battle?
8. Is mercy different than forgiveness? If so, how?
9. Have you acted nice to someone who was mean to you?
10. What kind of heart do you have toward God; tender, loyal, foolish, angry or submissive? Perhaps you can think of another word of how you feel about God.
11. How does a heart attitude toward God influnce a person's choices?
12. How can God help you to make better choices?

Allon

Book 9

In
Plain Sight

Shawn Lamb

Allon Books

Book 9 - Overview

Being the last book in the *Allon* series, there are many Spiritual themes explored, only in a unique way. In *Allon Book 1*, Dagar had already fallen and ruled by using the Dark Way. His character was established as being prideful and evil. In *Allon Book 9 – In Plain Sight*, I take a more personal approach to the subject by making Kell the focal point. As Jor'el's Captain of the Guardians, Kell is a strong, benevolent champion of right. His sudden and unexpected transformation into a mortal is meant to stun the reader as much as it does him. After all, who would expect Kell to even come close to exhibiting the same troubling personality flaws as Dagar?

Through Kell, the story unfolds by exploring man's weaknesses from a different perspective of the heavenly versus the earthly. Scripture says how angels are curious about man and about our relationship to God and redemption (1 Peter 1:13). Kell must not only adapt to the change, but also face challenges to his new life with accusations of crimes he didn't commit.

The main Biblical themes are pride and self-control. From these flow sorrow, grief and bitterness in contrast to compassion and sacrifice. For example, those who tend to be prideful are often not very compassionate to those around them. The flipside is those who display a tender heart of compassion, generally act without pride.

A person must have a slight amount of self-consideration in order to care for oneself. For example, everyone takes a certain amount of time to be cleaned, groomed and fed. Even Scripture makes this comparison when commanding a man to love his wife:

Ephesians 5:29

For no one ever hated his own flesh, but nourishes and cherishes it, just as Christ does the church.

There is no sin in caring for one's own needs. However, an imbalance of this self-consideration leads to *pride*, which was Lucifer's primary sin that guided all his subsequent actions.

Isaiah 14:14

I will ascend above the height of the clouds. I will make myself like the Most High.

Compassion is best outlined in

Philippians 2:3

Do nothing from selfish ambition or conceit, but in humility count others more significant than yourself.

Also from the heavenly perspective, several Biblical truths dealing with prophecy of the end times are touched upon. How will Jesus' coming affect angels and man? What role will believers play in the Millennium kingdom?

The Characters in Book 9
Central to the Theme

KELL – Time is drawing near for the Guardians' complete restoration to governing and Jor'el's return to Allon. It is a time Kell looked forward to, or at least he thought so.

Slowly and almost unknowing, the centuries impacted him in a negative way. Kell doesn't see it even when confronted by his fellow Guardians. Instead, he scorns the mortals he is supposed to serve and protect. To Kell, it's simply his role as captain.

In the events that follow Kell's transformation into the mortal *Kelvin*, I use this new perspective to give a glimpse into the differences between a spiritual viewpoint and earthly expectations. While everything is a mystery, Kell is constantly making comparisons between his Guardian life and a mortal existence.

At every turn, Kell is challenged to rethink his understanding. In relationships with mortals, he experiences love, rejection and jealousy, while trying to reassess his faith toward Jor'el in a new manner. The instant access to Jor'el is gone, and he wrestles with understanding the Almighty's purpose in allowing this to happen to him. He also deals with accusations of crimes he didn't commit.

The most important concept he struggles with is *self-control*, an area he believed he mastered while serving as captain. Thus *pride* crept in and dulled his *compassion* towards those in his charge. Only after he loses everything does he realize the impact of his behavior.

As with Christians, it often takes a divine chastening to understand and accept God's working in our lives.

Hebrews 12:5-6

My son, do not regard lightly the discipline of the Lord, nor be weary when reproved by Him. For the Lord disciples the ones He love, and chastises every son whom He receives.

Hebrews 12:5-6

Humble yourselves, therefore, under the mighty hand of God, so that at the proper time he may exalt you.

VIVIAN – In many ways, she shows the tender heart of compassion without pride. She is a compassionate nurse aiding her brother as an assistant in his medical profession. Also, she exhibits unselfishness in giving up on marriage to help Lester raise his young sons after he became a widower. She shows a gracious strength in her compassion when confronting Kell while he is in her care, and speaking to Wess in regards to his withdrawal from life's hardships.

WESS – Emotionally wounded from years of hardship and loss, he masks his feelings on difficult subjects with sarcasm and banter. Trouble in the South Plains is compounded by the arrival of *Kelvin*, who Wess sees as a rival for Vivian's affection.

The escalation of tension and jealousy between he and *Kelvin*, finally spurs Wess into action, both in regards to confessing his long-held love for Vivian and dealing with the crime wave plaguing the South Plains. For Wess, this catalyst helps him deal with the pain of his past and move on toward the future.

LESTER desperately wants Vivian to have a future, and is willing to sacrifice the truth of his illness. The bond of family love is displayed by brother and sister throughout the story.

AYERS – Bitterness from the past consumed him, and as such, he becomes the shell of the person he once was. He allowed his family to fall apart without regard for the final consequences.

ARMUS – Usually strong-minded and self-contained, Armus is overcome by sorrow and grief that affects his behavior and relationship to those around him. Unchecked emotion nearly leads to an unthinkable end for the mighty Guardian lieutenant. Shock and humiliation brings him back from the brink.

AVATAR – In contrast to Armus, Avatar suppresses his feelings, which are manifested in the bolstering of others in neglect of his own emotional health. Both forms of grief (Armus and Avatar) can be unhealthy, as neither acknowledges the cause thus avoids dealing with the emotions in a positive manner. At critical times, they are forced to come to terms with their feelings of loss and the future.

FITCH & LOCAN know the end is near since the laying of the cornerstone for Jor'el's Palace will signal the return of the Almighty. With the attitude of fallen angels, they vow to create as much chaos, trouble, death and destruction as possible before their ultimate demise.

JOR'EL – Throughout the series, Jor'el has been a representation of God. The prophecy of Jor'el's return is similar to the hope of Christians anticipating Christ's Second Coming. It signals the end to all suffering from the hard-fought battle and the final demise of Satan's reign on earth.

THE ROYAL FAMILY – The changing roles of Tyrone, Nigel and the House of Tristan represent the roles of Believers during the earthly Millennium Kingdom, which serves as a transition to the eternal kingdom.

Suggested Questions
Allon - Book 9

(Feel free to make your own questions.)

1. Have you said nasty things about someone? Why?
2. Could pride or bitterness be the reason you acted mean toward that person?
3. Have you ever been falsely accused of doing something wrong?
4. No one likes punishment, but do you understand why it is important? Read Hebrews 12:5-11 and discuss it with your parents
5. Can you think of someone else falsely accused of crimes and punished? Read Matthew 27:11-26. How do you feel about what He did for you?
6. How did Kell handle the limited access to Jor'el through prayer when he didn't receive an immediate answer? Can you accept delayed answers?
7. Did Kell succeed in learning his lessons? How?
8. Can you do like Kell and submit to God in changing bad behavior? Read 2 Peter 1:3-8.
9. Have you ever felt so sad that it changed the way you acted toward others?
10. Is someone you know acting angry or bad because of sorrow? If so, how can you help them?

Allon Series Overview

THE OBJECTIVE OF THE ENTIRE SERIES is to convey Biblical and spiritual principles to young people in such a way as make them come alive. Often, as kids get older, the Bible stories told in Sunday school classes grow stale, but *not* due to the Scripture, heaven forbid!

Scripture doesn't water down anything; not sin, not the fatal flaws of those Godly men and women in the Bible. Rather curriculum used for Sunday school distills the stories too much and tends to sanitize them for the children. This might work for the very young, but as children get older, they should see the fullness of the Biblical accounts. Allegory is a way to grab attention.

Yet, for a moment, let me be clear: I never have and never will claim my stories are near the authority of Scripture! NEVER! An imperfect creature can't write perfection. The Bible should trump any and all other forms of communication. What God has done, is given me the talent and ability to tell stories that can be used to help enforce principles and precepts. Thus, by His grace, I've written each story with certain Spiritual themes in mind and outlined those in this booklet.

The two major overarching themes of the series are:

1. Hope in Jor'el (God)
2. Jor'el (God) is in total control no matter how bleak the situation.

The Bible is filled with examples of hope, which also is counted as *faith*. Read Hebrews 11 about all the great men and women of *faith* who acted with *hope* based upon God's word and character.

71

The word *hope* appears from 130-150 times in Scripture depending upon the translation: King James or NIV. The Greek word primarily used in the New Testament is *elpis* meaning *expectation* or *confidence*. Various forms of Hebrew words in the Old Testament also carry the meaning of confidence and expectation.

Words used to describe *control* aren't really found in Scripture; however, God constantly warns about His *power*, and carries out His power with miracles. From Genesis 1:1 to Revelation 22:21 God's power and sovereignty is on display. In fact, God refers to Himself by the expression *I Am* over 6,000 times in Scripture. The Hebrews translated it YHWH (Yahhew) and the Greeks, Jehovah. Both terms mean *the self-existing one.* There is no doubt as to what God means when declaring *His Sovereignty.*

To help in understanding the series overview, here are a few suggested questions and activities. These are a bit more involved than earlier questions to provoke thought and discussion.

Suggested Questions and Activities
For the Allon Series

1. In Allon Book 1, what question did Jor'el ask Ellis while he was recovering in the infirmary at Melwynn? Do you have times of doubt? Why?
2. How did Owain's bad decision affect his family in *Insurrection*? Have you ever made a bad choice that hurt someone else? How did you rectify it?
3. As the *Heir Apparent*, Nigel felt a great weight of responsibility. Why didn't Nigel tell his father about his bad dreams? What does Scripture say about fear?
4. Can you think of a king in Scripture who played favorites with his children like Ellis did in *A Question of Sovereignty*? What happened?
5. What miracle did Jor'el perform in *Gauntlet* that Hueil could not? How did it affect those who witnessed it? Can you think of a similar incident in Scripture?
6. Why did Jor'el place a curse upon the Sorens? What *Dilemma* did the Guardians face as a result of this curse? Are men and women equal in the sight of God? Find a verse to support your answer.
7. What was the underlying sin that made Titus defy his father and sneak aboard the ship bound for Natan in *Dangerous Deception*? How did Tyrone display this same underlying sin? What did it take to resolve and heal the rift between father and son?
8. In *Divided*, what responsibility did Nigel finally accept that he avoided before? How did the events of his life prepare him to accept the crown? Is there something you are avoiding that God wants you to do? How can you prepare for that responsibility?

9. During the last book *In Plain Sight*, Jor'el deals harshly with Kell by turning the captain into a mortal. Why? How does Kell deal with the personal issues? What does Scripture say about the sin of pride?

10. How did Jor'el manifest his presence during the series? When did God appear as such in the Bible?

11. What did the Guardians and Shadow Warriors teach you about spiritual warfare? If you need help, read Romans 8:31-36 and Ephesians 6:10-13.

12. For each book, make a list of incidents that showed Jor'el as sovereign and in control of everything. Then mark which ones were for judgment and which ones were for help. What can such acts by God in the Bible tell you about Him?

13. Make a royal family tree starting with Ellis. What does Scripture say children are? How does that relate to Ellis' family? To your family?

14. Choose a mortal character that impacted you the most and write a biography. Once done, consider how that character changed overtime, what he/she learned and how it changed their life.

15. Can you think of Scriptures to illustrate the change of that mortal character? How can those Scriptures apply to you?

OTHER BOOKS BY SHAWN LAMB

Young Adult Fantasy Fiction
ALLON ~ BOOK 1
Published by Creation House, a division of Charisma Media

Published by Allon Books

ALLON ~ BOOK 2 ~ INSURRECTION
ALLON ~ BOOK 3 ~ HEIR APPARENT
ALLON ~ BOOK 4 ~ A QUESTION OF SOVEREIGNTY
ALLON ~ BOOK 5 ~ GAUNTLET
ALLON ~ BOOK 6 ~ DILEMMA
ALLON ~ BOOK 7 ~ DANGEROUS DECEPTION
ALLON ~ BOOK 8 ~ DIVIDED
ALLON ~ BOOK 9 ~ IN PLAIN SIGHT
THE ACTIVITY BOOK OF ALLON

For Young Readers – ages 8-10
Allon ~ The King's Children series
NECIE AND THE APPLES
TRISTINE'S DORGIRITH ADVENTURE
NIGEL'S BROKEN PROMISE

Historical Fiction
GLENCOE
THE HUGUENOT SWORD

Non-fiction
WRITING FICTION GOD'S WAY

Explore the Kingdom of Allon

www.allonbooks.com

Featuring:

- Read excerpts of Allon books
- Original Character Art
- Interactive Map of Allon
- News and Events
- Photo and Video Gallery
- Links to:
  - Facebook - The Kingdom of Allon Page
  - Contact Shawn Lamb

www.ingramcontent.com/pod-product-compliance
Lightning Source LLC
Chambersburg PA
CBHW071844020426
42331CB00007B/1845